Blue Amber:
A Glimpse in the Life of Amber Snyder

Guided Journal Version I

By: Amber Snyder

Created With:

Summer Ross

Cover Art by Vibrant Design

ISBN 979-8-9887052-0-8

Contents

Preface

In the midst of several hospitalizations, I decided I would help others like me. At the time of my resolution, I had no clue as to when or how I would do this. In 2015, during my second to last hospital stay in Washington DC, I figured I would start my own business collaborating with organizations that offer resources to underserved communities. It is my dream to open wellness centers for caregivers of individuals with noncommunicable diseases.

So, the entrepreneurship journey began with me brainstorming for a couple of years, but it was not until 2017 when I started writing down my ideas and goals. The following year I began attending events for small business owners. Along the way, in 2019, I registered a business in DC and attended workshops at DCRA to learn more about operating a small business and obtaining government contracts. This process is not for the faint of heart. I work a full-time job, and do not have the time to spend running around accomplishing little bits of nothing, which is how I felt most of 2019. Then COVID-19 hit and my plans to start a business were on pause. I could no longer attend in person workshops, and I did not find much online for DC small businesses. I was frustrated, feeling defeated and ready to give up on the idea until I had some conversations with my father. He encouraged me to be courageous and to start sharing my life experiences. After several phone calls with my dad, I toyed around with the idea and thought if my life was interesting enough to my dad and whoever he talks to about me, maybe he was on to something. I started thinking and could not name any other Black female with my condition who had traveled across the globe. A Black female living in China did not seem foreign to me because I was not the only in the cohort to travel to China.

I re-evaluated my life and thought my story may provide insight to and/or impact others in a positive way. I continue to struggle with starting a business and sharing my story, even as I write these words. I decided to tap into the connections I made on LinkedIn and in DC, and this led me towards writing. I contemplated writing blogs and returning to social media platforms. However, I chose a different route, as social media seems saturated to me. Around October of 2020, I attended a free workshop on becoming a published author called "Write and Publish." One of the facilitators offered a one-on-one session for the attendees. I found myself signing up for the free one-hour consultation over the phone. The coach mentioned I should write my memoir first. She suggested that writing and publishing first could potentially lead me to the connections I needed to bring my business idea to fruition.

I had already declared I would return to the hospitals with my heart set to inspire those who are ready to give up on life due to mental health issues. I recalled my desire to improve the treatment of Black females surviving with mental health and wellness. While locked in the hospital I dreamed of the day I could return and assist nurses, doctors, phlebotomists, ambulance drivers and others with improved treatment and care for mental health patients. I went as far as wanting to work with pharmaceutical companies on creating drugs without side effects. I was and am feeling empowered to speak for the patients who did not fully recover, who are voiceless, who do not have support systems and are silenced because of stigma.

I was and am fortunate to have a strong support base. I want everyone in my situation who wants help to receive the help they seek. Along this journey I have had tough moments. I used to say in my mind I will be a face for mental health care. Being an advocate for all the other individuals I met and could not help is one reason I write my story today. I am also writing this book to inspire others along their journey, to be a support to those who have made up their minds to overcome obstacles like depression, grief, anxiety, paranoia, and the other titles that make us differently-abled human beings.

Throughout this writing process, I have learned from reflecting that I have held on to too many fears and let go of too many dreams because I did not see a direct path. I gained insight as I wrote my story openly and honestly. I made myself cry while writing, and I laughed too as I wrote. Both tears and laughter are outlets for me. I was never one to talk or share openly what I grappled with the last 21 years of my life. I have everyone at the hospitals, all the therapists, doctors, and the nurse practitioner to thank for treating me. Thank you to the cooks and the janitors at the facilities I stayed in. To my family and extended family, thank you for not giving up on me, thank you for accepting me when I could not accept myself. To my friends who know somewhat about my struggle and to those who had no clue, thank you all the same. To my cohort in China, my family and I especially thank you!

I did not know how much or how little to share. I wrote what came out. And in the words of my late granny, "that's all she wrote, and the pencil point broke…."

Guided Journal

YOUR GUIDE TO INNER HEALING

BLUE AMBER

A Glimpse in the Life of Amber Snyder

"CONNECT, ENVISION, AND FEEL AS YOU READ THIS MEMOIR."

Introduction

A person can change over a lifetime, molding and evolving themselves into the circumstances that made them who they are today. Who we were at sixteen is vastly different from who we become at twenty-five or thirty-nine. To tell you who I am is no small feat. For I am a combination of all those I have met along my journey; I am a daughter, I am a sister, I am a businesswoman, but most importantly, I am a Woman. As you are reading this, I may have already stepped into the next phases of being. Who I am is ever changing, but for now, I can share with you who I was as covered in this memoir.

Shortly before my family moved from our home in Cleveland, Ohio to relocate to Cleveland Heights, Ohio we painted the bedrooms. My family is full of creative individuals, and while I am still discovering my creativity and accepting my talent(s) my siblings have already done so. My older brother is great at drawing, my older sister has a way with painting, and my dad is great with words. The three of them created their masterpiece on the walls of my brother's and sister's rooms. The most memorable was a wall in my brother's room. The simple yet profound quotes are ingrained in my mind. The first quote was "Know Thyself." The second quote on his wall was "To Thine Own Self Be True." As a person overcoming anxiety, catatonia, and paranoia, I relearn myself after each obstacle or lapse with reality. To know myself is a continuous reflection on my life as it was and how I want it to be. My family relationships are strong, and even as we have grown apart, I love each member just the same. It is beautiful and painful parting with family as we have separated geographically and by life choices.

I am the first of my siblings to graduate high school, college, and graduate school, earning a Master of Business degree in 2008 from Baldwin Wallace University in Ohio. I obtained my second master's degree in International Studies from Concordia University of Irvine in California. Helping others is something I am passionate about, and I work towards creating businesses to help caregivers and their loved ones obtain access to resources they may not have had access to otherwise. I am the second of my siblings to establish my own business. I work to cultivate my business into a bountiful dream come true, and I maintain my day job.

By day, I work for an independent federal government agency based in Washington DC. In an effort to build my brand, I have started to engage at conferences as a speaker to spread the word on what has helped me with mental health in hopes of inspiring others. My first virtual speaking event is for a WomenTech Conference. While I have used Microsoft Teams for live communication with coworkers and colleagues, I feel both nervous and excited to speak live for up to 20 minutes and answer potential questions. This is huge for me, as public speaking is a fear for many, and while I aced a public speaking course during undergrad school I still feel jitters each time I talk in front of others. As a businesswoman I welcome the opportunity for speaking engagements, though I prefer smaller venues. So, speaking to a camera and potentially not seeing the audience and feeling the vibe in the room is going to be a new adventure for me.

As a triple threat (Black, Differently-abled, Female) I am regaining my self-esteem and learning to display confidence in who I am, what I overcame, and where I aspire to land in life. This memoir is written for me and for you. Throughout my life, I have been a caring person, and now I am learning to care for myself first. In the loving words of my dad, "I cannot help anyone if I cannot first help myself." I am positioning myself to create the life I want. My mental health has not deterred me from living a full life even though I encounter daily obstacles.

Amber a Precious Stone

THE ONLY GEMSTONE THAT PROVIDES A GLIMPSE INTO OUR PAST.

The first time I ever recalled feeling fear was at my old family home in Cleveland, Ohio which was owned by my matriarchal grandparents. My family lived there for a time before we moved away during the middle of the year when I was still in 5th grade. At the time, I shared a room with my younger sister, and to get there you had to pass through my older sister's room and then walk through a closet. Outside of my older sister's doorway was a hall with many other doorways, including the doorway to our shared family bathroom. One night I had to use the bathroom. Everyone was sleeping. I usually had no issues leaving my room, walking through the closet to my older sister's room. However, I did not make it out of her doorway for a long time. I stayed at the end of her bed near the doorway until I nearly peed my pajamas. I recall trying to wake my older sister up to walk me, but to no avail. I would have to muster up the courage to walk out on my own. Directly across the hall from the door with the window was the bathroom. I was so frightened by the thought of seeing someone through the glass of the door which led downstairs. I was convinced that someone was there even though I knew it was closed. I did not want to go to the bathroom, because I feared they would snatch me and take me. The more I settled on just going for it the more I had to pee. After freezing up for what felt like an hour, I finally ran to the bathroom and quickly turned on the light. Once I made it to the toilet, I told myself not to look at the door with the glass on my way back. When I left the bathroom, I left the light on for comfort. Returning through the pitch-black hall was too much to bear again.

THEME

Fear of things not seen

INSIGHT

Fear is not just being afraid of things not seen, but can be fear of something we are anticipating. To overcome it, we must face it.

ADVICE

Ways to help alleviate anxieties surrounding fear.

1. Take a time out
2. Deep Breathe
3. Face your fears (avoidance makes it worse)
4. Visualize a happy place.

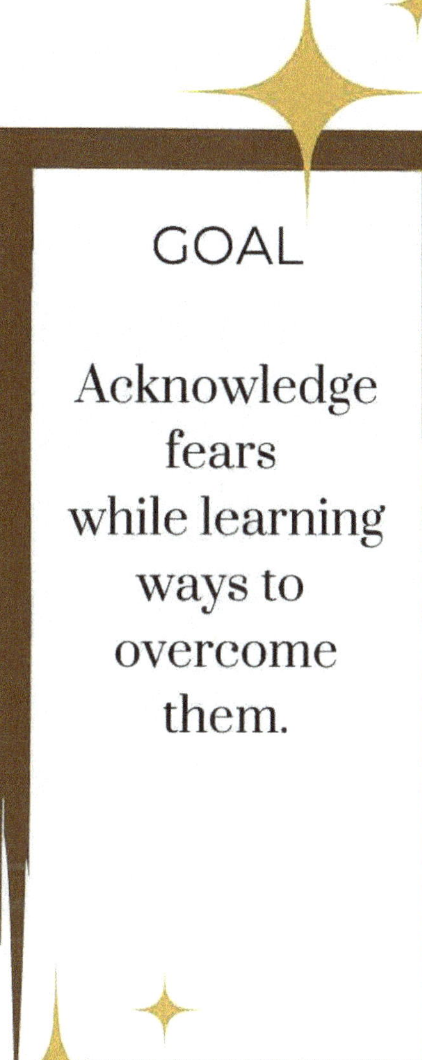

GOAL

Acknowledge fears while learning ways to overcome them.

"Do the thing you fear to and keep on doing it... that is the quickest and the surest way ever yet discovered to conquer fear."
~Unknown

Blue Amber

Journal Prompts:

HOW DID READING THIS CHAPTER MAKE YOU FEEL?

DO YOU HAVE ANY FEARS?

HAVE YOU OVERCOME THEM? IF SO, HOW DID YOU?

WHAT ADVICE WOULD YOU GIVE TO FRIENDS OR FAMILY WHO ARE TRYING TO OVERCOME A FEAR?

Weekly Journal

Weekly Journal

Blue Amber

NEWER TO THE GEM INDUSTRY. THOUGHT TO CALM THE MIND AND ALSO ALLEVIATE FEARS.

My grandparents also owned the house to the right of our home, which they rented out. One of the tenants was Mr. Teal. He had a white three-legged dog. The dog played in the backyard and was always attached to a makeshift leash that was just a rope tied from the garage across the yard and connected to the back of the house, like a clothesline. The dog could only hobble backwards or forwards in a single line as far as the leash would allow him. Needless to say, it was a sad sight to see. I often jokingly asked siblings and friends, "Why not put the dog out of its misery?" We would go on to say, "Why is Mr. Teal holding on to this poor dog?" Now, funny enough, pet owners purchase pet insurance! If there is that much love for a pet, how much more love is there for other human beings? Reflecting back, I learned a valuable lesson from Mr. Teal and his three-legged dog. Differently-abled beings are as loveable as all others. While this may not be an Ah-Ha moment to you, it definitely was to me. After my first mental health break, it took me two decades to start seeing value in myself.

For those curious minds who have never experienced a mental health break firsthand or second hand, I will explain what has happened to me. If I become overwhelmed, my sleep declines. Once I am not able to sleep (insomnia) I begin to overthink and the thoughts in my mind race. Racing thoughts feel like a mental adrenaline rush. Ever been on a roller coaster? Your nervousness builds as you ascend the ride. The closer you get to the point of descent, whatever you feel intensifies. Then as you drop, you may scream, feeling that deep knot in your stomach, and you close your eyes, bracing for the sudden rush. Well, the intense feeling you have, that lack of control over your body you have on the roller coaster ride is like the feeling I have in my mind when my thoughts race. I am not like the person on the ride who is able to throw up their arms and keep them up while descending.

Maybe you have never been on a roller coaster, but you have given a speech in front of peers, and internally your body kicks into automation; you feel your heart racing out of your chest, and you may sweat as the paper shakes in your hand, and you try to compose yourself but have no control over your body's reaction to your fear. That is what happens in my mind when I have racing thoughts. The thoughts become crippling to me. This sudden rush of information overloads my brain, and the ones I manage to process typically lead to me misinterpreting a situation or causing me to freeze. I literally have a plethora of thoughts at once, and I am unable to decide what to do. I go slower with my physical motions if I move at all. I am at my worst when I stop speaking, eating, and sleeping.

Recovering is a process of second guessing my thoughts and the situation or environment I am in. Once I am coming out of a trance, I seem paranoid and distrustful of my surroundings. The more I am around people who do not experience anxiety and intense fear, I become comfortable. The more at ease I am, the less I worry if my loved ones and I are safe. When the worry decreases, my thoughts slow down, and I decrease my doubts about my surroundings. I begin to make sense of my thoughts by expressing myself verbally and asking those close to me if I am okay. So, I seek external validation to reassure an internal sense of self. I know I am better when I no longer seek outside opinions for my internal feelings.

During my second mental health collapse, I recall coming down the stairs to the living room. My mom was there sitting in one of her orange chairs she kept from our old house in Cleveland. My sister was also in the living room. I saw her sitting at the table. As I reached the last step, I asked them to kill me. I was serious, as I no longer wanted to suffer from the side effects of the medication, and I felt I was too young to need medicine. I do not know how that impacted my mother. I do not recall any other conversations about it with her after she told me no. My older sister has a dark sense of humor. I cannot be certain, but I am pretty sure she laughed. Her back was turned to me, so I was not able to see her face to confirm. Once she realized my sincerity, she consoled me. My sister created a pallet on the living room floor. She dimmed the lights and played soothing music. She told me everything would be alright. My mother had already gone into the kitchen or a different room. Reflecting back, I like to think the thought of losing her middle girl was more than she wanted to think about. I believe she just got busy to block the thought, knowing life goes on. She may have gone and said a prayer to put it in God's hands.

My thoughts at times get the best of me. I think something and hold on to it. Then I create a story around it. 'What if' scenarios are what I call the stories. What if my parents signed up their five kids for some kind of government experiment for financial gain? You see, growing up, our family was an ideal model of a Black family. My dad, a brown-skinned man. My mom, a fair-skinned woman with light eyes. Together, they had five light-skinned kids, all with light eyes like my mother. Except for me, I had brown eyes like my dad. To see the seven of us together was a beautiful thing. We were constantly receiving compliments. These compliments I often ignored, thinking the kind words were for my siblings. I had brown eyes like most others. I was not unique by way of eye color, so I did not receive the compliments. I excluded myself based on my brown eyes.

Journal Prompts:

HOW DID READING THIS CHAPTER MAKE YOU FEEL?

HAVE YOU EVERY EXPERIENCED ANXIETY?

WHAT ARE SOME SELF-CARE TECHNIQUES THAT HAVE HELPED YOU IN THE PAST EASE YOUR ANXIOUS FEELINGS?

WRITE ABOUT A TIME YOU EXPERIENCED ANXIETY, AND HOW YOU OVERCAME IT.

Weekly Journal

Weekly Journal

THEME

Anxiety

INSIGHT

Anxiety will send our bodies into flight or fight mode. It can come from the stress of things unknown. Self-validation can be used as a tool

GOAL

Acknowledge anxiety while learning to assuage symptoms

ADVICE

Ways to help alleviate feelings of anxiety.

1. Stay active
2. Practice Mind-fullness
3. Practice deep breathing.
4. Prioritize self-care

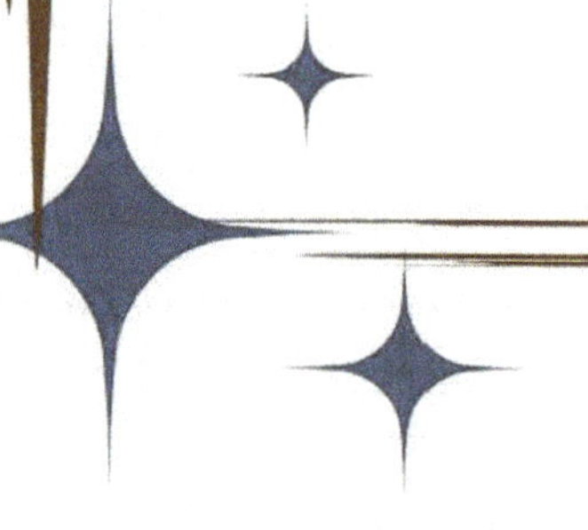

"Never let the future disturb you. You will meet it, if you have to, with the same weapons of reason which today arm you against the present."
~Marcus Aurelius

Blue Amber

Black Amber

SOME PEOPLE DENY IT EXISTS, OTHERS BELIEVE IT ABSORBS AND DISPELS NEGATIVE ENERGY.

My dad started his ministry pastoring a junior church in the basement of St. John AME. At this church is where I formed the thought that our family was an ideal model. You see, the government-assisted housing was across the street from our church. I did not learn about the projects or affordable housing until my dad's ministry. I knew to stay away from the area. Then there was Vacation Bible School (VBS). Kids from across the street were welcomed in. Not sure how or when, but the idea to invite the kids to service sprouted from leadership. Junior church service became more attended than the adult service upstairs. I considered church service with the adults dead or dull. Service in the junior church was not. To attract souls to Christ, my dad and other supporters had a theory that it was best to start with the youth. The parents may notice their children were attending and find their own needs met through the church. Attendance increased, and fellowship and true service began. As the church was able to meet the needs of the community, there was growth. Healing occurred between classes as worshiping together decreased fear and increased understanding. It was no longer 'don't go over there' but it 'was come as you are.' Junior church grew and friendships blossomed at our AME church. It was at this church I learned that not all families were a unit. My nuclear family was a unit, as my siblings had the same parents and we all lived together. At the time, I was young when my dad pastored the junior church. I realized not all families have two dependable parents dwelling in the home. The realization of different norms in family structures made me feel more aware of the world and less sheltered.

Our family spent countless hours at the church with other faithful, hardworking, God fearing members. I feel our family bonded as we watched the dynamics of the church flourish. We had cultural arts day, Easter egg hunts, Black nativity plays, Christmas plays, and concerts, to name a few activities outside of Bible study, youth choir, lock-ins, and trips to Wilberforce, a nearby historically Black college owned by the AME church network. Church became more than just service and Sunday school. Interacting with youth across the street opened my eyes to disparity. The kids, through no fault of their own, were in need. During that time, our church stepped up to meet their needs and reaped life in return. The doors of the church were open, and it opened my eyes to a new world.

Church could be fun and was not always dull. Each year there was a cultural awareness event. Each participant or family would represent a country of their choice and create a display. One year, my mom decided to represent an Asian country. She cooked Asian dishes and wore traditional

Asian attire. Others represented countries from Europe and Africa. It brought different cultures to life and enriched my mindset. I was open to trying new foods and interested in facts about places I never knew I would visit. It sparked my curiosity in differences and uniqueness amongst people. I would go on to meet older members who were attending graduate school to become doctors. I met lawyers and others in successful roles or on their way to achieving great things.

Sapphire accepted me as her goddaughter. She would babysit for my parents here and there. This was helpful to my parents and beneficial for me as well. I could sometimes spend the night at her place with my younger sister. She continued to be a guiding force in my life, and someone I looked up to outside of my family.

My father continued growing his ministry in the AME church, following in his dad's steps. My grandfather was a pastor in the AME church. He also worked in construction as an entrepreneur. My grandmother was a first lady. My mom became a first lady when my dad took his first head pastor role within the AME church. My parents both worked construction. My dad's churches were never megachurches. I like to think small church assignments were a good thing for my dad because he would have more time for his family. As an adult I see how the childhood memories of church have had a major influence on my life. Being raised in church makes me feel I always have a safe haven. Church proves the saying: raise a child in the way you want them to grow, if they stray, they always know they have a strong foundation to return to. The foundation for me is the Black church. I feel the church offers a sense of community, for all are welcome. The lessons I learned then still impact me today. I know no matter how hard things get, I can turn to believers for support and encouragement. Showing love to others and being kind and decent are beliefs that shaped who I am today.

My parents wanted to give their children the best chance in life. In Cleveland, my dad did not see a bright future for his five kids. He would do things like talk to our bus driver to keep track of us. My older brother and sister did not want to take the bus to school. My older brother rarely wanted to be on the school bus. He wanted to walk or ride his bike to school. The two oldest being together made my dad feel worse. He had double worries that something bad would or could happen to them, and it increased the risk for them to get into trouble – or worse – killed. My dad got in good with the bus driver, Miss B. Miss B rocked a jerry curl and a leather jacket. She took no mess. Her bus was full and quiet in the morning and in the afternoon. She was a no-nonsense type of person but still cool. She cared for the kids and it showed. She had no problem informing my dad when my brother and sister were not on her bus. The exchanges between Miss B and my dad led to him whooping his four eldest children together. He learned that we covered for each other. I guess his arm grew tired of giving all four of us whoopings because lectures became his disciplinary tool. As a pastor, my dad can talk. His long-windedness was more painful than the whooping. He would lecture us for hours it seemed. Our parents were overprotective, and I later learned why. I used to think they did not understand us being kids and wanting to have fun. I was wrong. They understood well the dangers lurking around from sketchy adults to troubled youth.

Our parents set geographical boundaries for how far my siblings and I could go in our neighborhood. For example, we were not permitted to pass Royal's grandmother's house, which was around the corner from our home. If we went down the street towards Superior, a main road, we were not to pass our older brother's friend's grandmother's house. We spent so much time outside in our youth during the summer. There were youth day camps we attended at Karamu House. We would walk or bike to Case Western Reserve University for math and science programs. After those activities let out, we would play in the backyard. There were grapevines in the backyard on the fence that produced concord grapes. We would eat the grapes by squeezing the center out of the skin, since we could not run in and out of the house to rinse them off with water.

I remember spending time on the sideline while my older brother played on Pal Five's football team for the Pee Wee League. My older sister was a cheerleader for the team, and my mother was a coach. My younger sister was aspiring to become a cheerleader as she stayed front and center on the sideline watching the cheerleaders practice. At the end of one football practice my brother came off the field to have a hot dog and drink an orange pop. There was a bee on his pop can. My brother did not see, and I guess no one else did besides me. I was quiet and did not yell or scream. I watched him drink the pop. I hoped the bee would have flown away as he tilted the can to take a gulp. It did not fly away. It stung my brother on the tongue. It took me years to share with him that I saw that bee. His football team was good. Pal Five made it to the championship two years in a row. We traveled with the team to Florida for the championship game twice. This was great fun because we went to Disney World two summers in a row.

Our family did not only travel to Florida together, we went to Niagara Falls several years in a row. Once my dad took us to see the Falls and had us so close to the edge as to get the view of the water in the picture. The waterfall was not the only reason we traveled to Canada. There were cultural festivals called the Caribbean. These celebrations were islanders who came from all over the world. Watching the dancers move to the beat of the drummers while parading down the streets with decorated costumes and floats was amazing.

Winter months allowed us time to build forts in the front yard and have snowball fights. I do not remember building snowmen. And the funny thing about building forts for snowball fights is my dad would always say to us "we are in a war" and "playtime is over" during his lectures. His statements make way more sense now than they did when I was a child. The irony of what he'd state are evident in the face of police brutality and a system still based on racism in the 21st century, with sentiments of hatred and disdain yet prevalent today. Always well intentioned, my dad's delivery did and still does come across as harsh and forceful.

I have fond memories of the first home I recall in Cleveland.

I never wanted to move from my home in Cleveland. My parents up-rooted our family and relocated us to more affluent neighborhoods – we were a middle-class family, and they wanted to give us the best opportunities available. I did not think our neighborhood in Cleveland was so bad. We would hear gunshots every so often; however, it was not the norm to hear gunshots. I was more afraid of jumping in the water during swim lessons and swim meets than I was afraid of the gunshots.

It is still a mystery why I did not want to jump in the water at swim practice. I was so afraid to jump and would refuse to do so. I was an excellent swimmer. I remember coming in second or third place sometimes. This was surprising for some, seeing how I would not dive into the pool with my opponents. I started myself at a disadvantage by not jumping or diving in. That is what my coach, Maroon, at Tri-C downtown campus would say. He tried to convince me to jump in. During practice I started to come out of the locker room late. I wanted to miss the part where our team, the Barracudas, formed a single line to dive in. Maroon must have noticed. Coach had this deep baritone voice. He was very loud, and when he yelled you could see his big belly and chins vibrate in sync. Either Maroon had confidence, or he did not care about appearances. I say this because he rarely wore a shirt during practice. Our team was coed, and we loved our coach. I never understood why he did not mind his belly showing. Now, I see he was not insecure about his body, which is a wonderful lesson on body confidence for the youth he coached. Anyway, that deep voice of his carried far back into the girls' locker room. He would yell to me and the others to make it out on time. I figured out if I was at the end of the jump in the pool line, he could not spend too much time trying to make me jump, as he had to get on with practice. I would even begin the swim meets already in the pool, holding on to the side and push off to start swimming. No one understood what that was about, and I did not care. Now, the exception made for me to start in the pool is known as a reasonable accommodation. The coach had to lobby to the officials on my behalf.

I never thought about how others may have perceived me. Those spectators in the crowd probably wondered why I was in the pool. My opponents likely thought I did not know swim meet protocol. Our Barracuda's team was all Black swimmers, and maybe that alone was a sight to see. There is a common misconception that Black people do not know how to swim. So, my fear of jumping in may have sparked curiosity, or maybe no one even noticed, as I do not recall outsiders saying anything about it directly to me. There was a deaf person on our team as well. He was dope. He mastered every swim stroke, and butterfly was his best style. Maybe when Coach Maroon explained about the deaf teammate, he slid my need in too. My parents and others who knew me inquired if it was the feeling of water in my ears, or the water and chlorine in my eyes. My sisters wondered if the fear was due to getting my hair wet.

My mom and my sisters knew how difficult it was to wash my hair in the bathtub. It was a struggle for my mom. I challenged her every time and never adjusted to her washing my hair. My mom refused to allow me and my two sisters to get our hair relaxed. I did not have my first relaxer until high school. My mom was old school. She pressed our hair with the hot comb. If it was not a special occasion, she would braid our natural hair. When my mom was not available to braid our hair, she left it to my dad. My dad was much gentler when doing our hair. Maybe he feared if he combed too hard our hair would fall out. Whatever the case, he would add the grease to our hair. I will never forget how he used the pink stuff called Luster's moisturizing oil. After rubbing the pink stuff in his hands, he would start from above the eyebrows and slap my forehead and then slick it back to my hair to form the ponytail. Here and there, my sisters and I still laugh about those moments of our dad doing our hair. I do not know for sure, but maybe he started at the forehead because he forgot he was not in church service anointing our heads with oil.

Second funniest hair story is when I would try to press my bangs myself. One time I did, and the hot comb was too hot. I burned my bangs. I did not burn them out. It was just enough for the burnt hair smell to fill the kitchen. It was in the morning before I was to head out for school. My older sister came in the kitchen and asked if I tried to do it myself. I lied and told her no. She said, "Amber, I smell the burnt hair and I see where your bangs are singed." She pulled the burnt strands so I could see what she was seeing. Then she showed me how to test the hot comb on a white paper towel first. She said if it browns the paper towel to blow the hot comb and wave it so the comb cools down. We still laugh about it sometimes. More so, because she knows I am a bad liar. Even by omission I do not lie well. I tell the truth or keep quiet.

I hated getting my hair washed and pressed. I was afraid of my scalp getting burned, and the heat of the comb just made me clench up every single time the hot comb came close. My mom was good at getting close, and I do not actually remember her burning me once. I was just tender-headed and knew what could happen if she did burn me. I never did pinpoint the fear of jumping in the water. I know I did not start jumping in until summer after 5th grade when we moved away from our home in Cleveland.

Journal Prompts:

HOW DID READING THIS CHAPTER MAKE YOU FEEL?

THINK BACK ON ONE OF THE HAPPIEST MOMENTS YOU'VE EXPERIENCED. DESCRIBE IT. WHO WAS WITH YOU? WHY WAS THIS MOMENT SPECIAL TO YOU?

WHO CAN YOU DEPEND ON AS A LISTENING EAR?

WHAT QUALITIES DO THESE PEOPLE POSSESS THAT MAKES THEM GREAT LISTENERS?

Weekly Journal

Weekly Journal

THEME

Who and What Shaped us

to be who we are today

INSIGHT

Connecting back to our roots can not only help us learn who we are, but can show us appreciation for those who helped us be who we grew to be.

ADVICE

1. When we lose sight of who we are, look back at where we came from.
2. Call up a close friend or family member for a quick conversation.
3. Show those around you gratitude, cook them a nice meal, take them out for a little bit.
4. Learn your love languages, not just for romantic relationships, but for friendships too.

GOAL

Show readers gratitude, and show them that there are people here for them, in times of need.

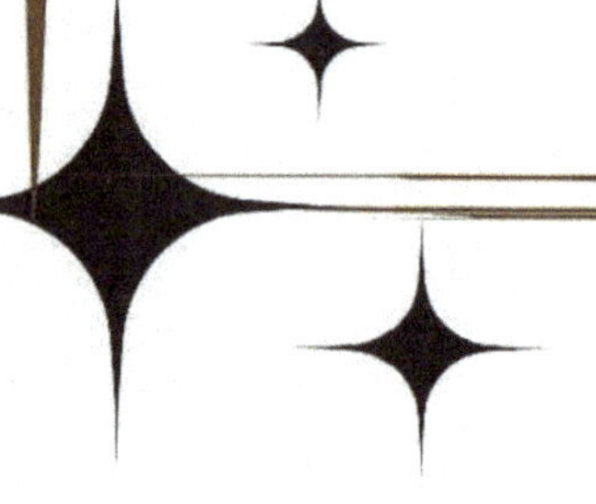

"Family and Friendships are the greatest facilitatators of happiness."
--John C. Maxwell

Blue Amber

Green Amber

POPULAR AND MORE BEAUTIFUL AS IT BECOMES MORE TRANSPARENT. IT IS SAID TO HAVE PROPERTIES OF HEALING VARIOUS KINDS OF STRESS.

The holidays were intense then. I do not know how my mom cooked so much food for so many relatives. Thanksgiving at home was full of laughter and card games. My sisters and I had to set the table for Thanksgiving dinner, and we were assigned chores to help out with cleaning up. When we were deemed old enough, my mom allowed us to make desserts. The favorite recipes for desserts were the pies. The recipes were from my mom's side of the family: pecan pie and what we call oatmeal pie. Oatmeal pie is still a personal favorite of mine.

There were movie nights with the seven of us at the time. Whoever had popcorn duty risked a whooping if it was burnt. There was not microwave popcorn back then. We had to pop it on the stove. There was a technique to putting the butter on as not to make the popcorn too soggy. When the butter is too hot it causes the popcorn to feel and look prechewed. Even to this day, I pop my popcorn on the stove. I guess doing so is nostalgic for me.

All these memories and more may provide insight into how I internalize my environment. It might also shed light on why I am very observant. Not expressing myself and excluding myself creates a disconnect. I am not always inclined to provide real time input. Meaning correction of misinterpretation was/is not available. I held/hold it all in. Is it possible I misconstrued my reality starting well before my first mental break? I do not know, as I thought I was normal. I thought my life was normal growing up. My nuclear family seemed normal. Until life started to happen, and I became more exposed to the way the world is.

I attended several different schools before we moved. I remember a Christian school the most. This school was the least diverse in demographics. Back then, paddling in school was allowed. My parents signed off that to paddle us was acceptable. Paddling by someone outside of my family scared me. I behaved and never received paddling. I always felt sorry for the kids who did. For those who do not know what paddling is, let me explain. Say a student misbehaves or does something wrong. That student could be called to the principal's office. Sometimes the child is given a chance to share their side of what or why an action happened. The principal or assistant principal then determines the punishment. If it is deemed paddle-worthy the child received a whooping. Not with a belt or hand, but with a flat, wide, wooden handheld device. The handle was short, and the other end was longer and wider than the handle. It was usually a light tan color. Think of a paddle used for boating. It is the same kind of mechanism only not as long.

Before this school, I interacted minimally with non-Black students, teachers, and leaders. At the Christian school, in 2nd grade, I recall the teacher placing me in an advanced math group. The same teacher did not assign me to an advanced reading group. A student, also in advanced math, said, "You should be in advanced reading too." He disagreed with the teacher on my reading ability. He believed I belonged in the advanced group. I remember this moment. He wanted me to stand up for myself. To tell the teacher she was incorrect. To show her that I should be in the more advanced group for reading. I did not stand up for myself. I did not challenge my authority, the teacher. I was raised to respect my elders and not to challenge my authorities. That was all good and well when my elders and authorities were also Black, with my best interest at heart. Like I said, this was my first time interacting with non-Black students, teachers, and leaders. I trusted her over myself and my classmate. Why did I not take my classmate's advice and challenge her? I wish I had. I still have doubts about sounding out words properly. The teacher may also have had some bias.

When I was in 3rd grade at the same school, this same teacher slapped my younger sister who was in 2nd grade. The teacher claimed my younger sister spit on her. My siblings and I were taken out of the school. My parents were no longer willing to pay after the incident. There is a difference between abuse and discipline. My dad's belt "razor" as he called it, was used to discipline and correct behavior. The paddle was deemed a way of correction. The slap was abuse.

I encountered my first and only disciplinary action in school when we moved to Cleveland Heights. We left our single-family home in Cleveland to live in a duplex on Sycamore. I feel I shared the same sentiment as my mom about moving. We did not want to relocate. My mom neither liked moving nor change. I did not like the unknown. I did not want to leave my friends. It was the middle of 5th grade. Wintertime at that. The elementary school I attended when we moved to Cleveland Heights was called Boulevard. This school went up to grade five. Most of the kids had known each other from prior grades. I had to make myself accepted. I was joining mid school year. The 5th graders were at the top of the school. Meaning, they set the examples and were looked up to by those in younger grades. Entering a new elementary school and not knowing anyone, starting all over making new friends, was challenging.

There was a time some students would tease me about my lips. Not just me but another girl too. The students would say we had fish lips. Being taunted about my facial features did not phase me, as I knew from older cousins that my other features would grow in, and my face would become more symmetrical. Also, my older cousins told me how men like big lips and that I would see when I got older. At the time I never felt ugly, but I never felt beautiful either, as looks were not yet important to me. I was raised with the notion that beauty is only skin deep, and I take to heart the Temptations song about beauty.

One afternoon, the bell rang for school to let out. I was finishing up an assignment with a classmate. I snatched something from him. Taking my Trapper Keeper from him upset him. He was so mad he called me the B word. Without hesitation, I slapped him in the face. I am slow to anger until I am pushed, but he crossed the line trying to make me feel less than who I was by disrespecting me. I could handle the teasing about my lips, but to deliberately attack my character is a different story. Those were fighting words. As bad as saying "yo momma" to someone back in the day. We began to tussle, and the teacher had to separate me from him. She wrote the two of us up. This meant we had to spend the day in the pink room together. The pink room at Boulevard was in-school suspension. This was the worst, because I missed a field trip on the day we were in the pink room. I did not understand why they forced two students who fought each other to sit in the same room all day. The funny thing about it is by lunch, I was so bored I attempted to make amends with him. He must have been just as bored, because he accepted. We chatted the remainder of the day for entertainment. Being in the pink room was the first and last time I was disciplined in school. I do not think my parents were aware of the incident. In fact, I am pretty sure they were not, as I would have remembered receiving a punishment at home too.

See, my parents were strict. They wanted us focused on doing well academically. We could not even have the landline phone number to our house, as our parents did not want outsiders calling us all the time. It was by accident that I discovered the phone number. It was one evening around dinner. Our parents ordered Papa John's pizza. On the side of the pizza box, I found a phone number beneath our address. I informed my siblings, and together we figured out how to check if it was our house number. We used our neighbors' phone to check if the phone rang to our house. Indeed, it was the house number, and we were in business. Our parents, amused and yet not pleased at our discovery, set parameters around when we could receive calls.

Journal Prompts:

HOW DID READING THIS CHAPTER MAKE YOU FEEL?

WHAT THINGS DO YOU DO WELL?

WHAT DOES FEELING SELF-ASSURED MEAN TO YOU?

NAME 5 THINGS THAT YOU LOVE ABOUT YOURSELF.

Weekly Journal

Weekly Journal

THEME

Self-Esteem & Self Awaeness

INSIGHT

Reconnecting with your inner self and beliefs can improve your confidence.

ADVICE

What things can help improve your self esteem?
1. Step out of your comfort zone
2. No negative self-talk.
3. Forgive yourself for things not talked about and past actions.
4. Celebrate your wins even the small ones. 5. Create daily affirmations ("I am ")

GOAL

Positive self-refections.

"I am the measurer of my worth, and I say I am worthy" ~Unknown

Blue Amber

Red Amber

VERY AUTHENTIC COLOR. USED TO GET OUT OF STAGNATION AND TO FILL YOU WITH POSITIVE ENERGY.

Cleveland Heights was a diverse community. I did not make friends during my 5th grade year at Boulevard. The popular girls were not too fond of me. See, there was a girl who was the pretty girl, and her ex-boyfriend had a crush on me. This caused me to be disliked and not accepted at Boulevard. I had friends on my street, Sycamore, so it did not trouble me as much being disliked at school. I was in a loving home, and I still had fun after school. Plus, my sisters were there for me. Well, that is until division started, as my older sister was in 6th grade at Monticello. She, too, was having a hard time with other girls at her school. I am sure she was unafraid of the bullies who may have been jealous of her and the attention she received from boys in the school. My older sister, who is gorgeous and speaks her mind, was getting into fights and was transferred to Roxboro Middle School.

Summer came around and we played outside a lot. Our friends, my younger sister, sometimes my older brother, and rarely my older sister would go to Cumberland Pool. This pool is where I began jumping in the water and even doing cannonballs. Summer was a blast in Cleveland Heights. Our parents had a stronger sense of security and somewhat let their guard down. As long as we stuck together, we could explore our neighborhood more than we could at our old home.

Our neighbors in the duplex attached to our home were the Kaheems. They, too, were a large family, except they were grown adults. One of the neighbors was the landlord who lived in the duplex with his mom, and some of his siblings were in and out. At first it was nice to see and bond with their family. It made me think how close my own family could stay when we grew older. I remember summer nights sitting on our porch steps with our family and theirs. Their mom was Afrocentric. She also played music like Sade loud enough for us to hear while on the porch. My dad even took up playing the djembe after the neighbor. He got pretty okay at it, learning his rhythm and how best to position the drum itself. Prior to summer arriving, influenced by the neighbors, my parents partook in a spring cleansing where we ate nutritious foods and took natural herbs for a week straight. We did not eat meat or were not supposed to eat meat. My younger sister and I had some beef jerky here and there from the corner store. I did not feel guilty for eating meat during this time, as I never agreed to only eat healthy. That week, we still cleansed our bodies and learned the importance of eating healthy. The idea of 'eat to live, not live to eat' came to life for the first time that summer we did the spring cleansing. Our families really bonded.

The bond was broken when I came home to see my mom with a black eye. Initially I thought my dad hit her. I had all kinds of ideas swirling around in my mind. I felt confused and angry that someone hurt my mom. Then I discovered why my older sister was not around as much. I learned that she would have to go live with our uncle and cousins in Richmond Heights. When that did not keep this predator and molester away, she had to move to Youngstown with our grandmother. My sister's life was turned upside down due to no fault of her own. This happened the summer after I finished 5th grade. I hated him. Hated him because I had to move again from an area that I grew to love. Hated him because he changed my sister forever. Let alone, he had the audacity to hit my mother in the face. The humiliation our family faced, as it seemed the entire world knew my mom had a black eye and who the culprit was. My mom fought for my sister.

This became a family secret and was not talked about much after we moved away. I am not even sure my sister received professional assistance, and she bears the burden of such devastation to this day. She was not a black sheep, a badge she took on later in life. I suffered my first loss in Cleveland Heights....my sweet older sister. I learned more than I wanted to about some men. I learned why my parents attempted to guard us, as you just can never be too sure who is safe and who is not.

Crazy how sometimes it is not the perfect stranger who is sketchy. To this day our family rarely talks about the pain my sister endures. About how she must have felt and must feel having been separated from the fold of our family unit. Keeping it a family secret was to protect who? I now wonder. My sister and all of us bore the pain alone. Hindsight is 20/20 and I wish we had brought my sister in closer to our family and pressed charges against the perpetrator even without her statement(s). The situation directly impacted her for a lifetime and indirectly had negative impacts on our family. Not to speak of the situation, protect her, and be the voice for her would be double the pain for me if I were in her shoes. These situations are not uncommon, unfortunately. It is time to speak out and protect the innocence of our youth. Sometimes this is learned behavior, going untreated and destroying more lives. I say stop the silence and have the courage to be the needed voice.

Journal Prompts:

HOW DID READING THIS CHAPTER MAKE YOU FEEL?

HAVE YOU EVER EXPERIENCED GRIEF?

HAVE YOU EMBRACED THE LOSS SO YOU COULD LET GO EASIER?

WHAT THINGS HAVE ENCOURAGED YOUR HEALING JOURNEY?

Weekly Journal

Weekly Journal

Loss & Greif

INSIGHT

Loss and grief are tough things to experience. Try to remember the person you were before, and see where you are today as strength.

ADVICE

Coping with grief and loss
1. Recognize it won't feel like this forever.
2. Be gentle and patient with yourself.
3. Understand that you are not alone.
4.Journal about positive memories.

GOAL

Accept grief and loss. Not only a deceased loved one, a ended relationship or friendship.A loss of a job or opportunity.

"What we once enjoyed and deeply loved we can never lose, for all that we love deeply becomes part of us."
~Helen Keller

Blue Amber

White Amber

PRAISED FOR ITS NATURAL BEAUTY.

Again, I had to leave behind friends. This time it was even more difficult to adjust to the new living environment. Yes, we were now in a more affluent city. Yes, it seemed as though nights were quiet and schools were orderly. Moving from Cleveland to Cleveland Heights and now to Broadview Heights was devastating for me. I'd have to leave my old friends and make new friends all over again. My exposure to the way of the world grew, and the space we occupied decreased. We moved from a single-family, four-story home, as a middle-class family in an impoverished neighborhood where I was secure with my family as a unit, to a duplex where we were in a middle-class area as a normal family only to leave as a divided unit. Then we relocated as a middle-class family to a three-bedroom townhome apartment in an affluent white space. I had support at home in 7th grade but faded as I suffered more loss.

At the middle school, I was not mistreated, and I was not teased like at the elementary school in Cleveland Heights. I was simply ignored. To be the only Black and the only Black female in the school was the most isolating experience I have had to this day. I did not fit in, nor did I try to blend in. I would sit watching the clock most days. I did well as far as grades were concerned. Socially, I say I am still awkward as a result. The isolation I felt was only bearable when I made it to 9th grade, but 7th and 8th grade were tough. I had support at home, though even home was turbulent. My mother in her mid-thirties had what the doctors called a late onset of a mental health challenge. I lost my mom as I knew her. What happened to my mom is all I thought about for months. I was afraid for her and that I had lost her forever. I thought I needed to be strong and took on more than I needed to as a kid.

My siblings and I stayed over my grandmother's more and more during my mother's healing time. My grandmother must have felt how I worried and saw my concern. One day my grandmother said to me, "Amber, you must let go. I know you are worried about your mother. You need to let it go, as it is out of your control. You have to leave this in God's hands." She then told me to raise my arms and stretch them out with my hands facing palm up. I repeated after her, "Lord, I am leaving this to you, as there is nothing I can do." I felt her hand on the center of my back as she told me to inhale deeply and to hold my breath for a couple of seconds and then exhale. She had me repeat the breathing exercise with my arms still stretched out and palms facing up. My grandmother told me to do that every time I thought of my mom's situation.

Sometime in the 8th grade, my dad sat me down at the dining room table. He shared how he and my mom were going to separate, but that he would always be around. I did not realize the impact of divorce. At the time, I thought it was maybe due to my mom's illness, but it was more than that, and I did not see the signs leading to their divorce. I remember saying to my dad, "Do what is best for the two of you." I never heard my mom's side of the story as to why they were to separate. My dad kept his word and stayed around during my mom's healing. When he moved out of the apartment, I had mixed feelings. Then he brought me, my younger sister, and my baby brother to his home in Cleveland. During this short time, I attended Nathan Hale Middle School. I was happy to be away from Broadview Heights. I was back in my element with Black and brown students. The school was a mess to be frank. In comparison to the environment I'd left, the students were not learning, and there were endless disruptions caused by students who did not value or understand the importance of learning. The school had teachers and students who cared but were out-voiced by those who did not. I wanted to stay at the school because I had friends there. My dad was not having it. As soon as my mom was better and stable, we had to move back to our apartment. I finished the 8th grade back in isolation, but I kept in touch with my friends from my short adventure at the other school.

I was excited about starting high school, as I would no longer be the "only," meaning the only Black or brown person in the room or building for that matter. My siblings and a handful of other nonwhite students attended the high school. I became best friends with an Egyptian girl who took me under her wing and introduced me to her Italian friend. My brother was already friends with the Italian girl's brother. One summer I was at the Italian girl's home. She, her older brother, and I were in the kitchen. I was sitting at the table with my back to the door. Her brother's friend entered. They asked him how his interview went. Then without hesitation he said, "They gave the job to an N-word." Except he said the hard "N". The siblings started apologizing and I froze. He said "Oh, I did not see her there." That was my first time hearing the language in my face, and I did nothing. I internalized the situation. I took note of his face so I could later describe him to my older brother. I drank beer that day. I remained friends with the Italians but felt I could not trust any white person, as I felt they all conspired behind closed doors. I started to go out and even began to smoke weed the summer after freshman year.

This summer was fun until I suffered my second loss. At the time, my brother was heavily into rap, as were his friends. I was too. I had a shrine of Tupac on my wall. Every magazine picture I found of him, I would cut it out and tape to my wall. One day, I thought we were headed to a party. It was my older brother, his friends, and my older sister. We were two or three cars deep. One of the cars pulled off. The other two remained. My older brother was in a car in front of the car I was in. We had music playing, but I heard gun shots. I knew it was not the music. I still do not know why it happened. Both cars pulled off, and we drove to someone's apartment nearby. That night, our apartment was invaded by police and my brother was arrested. I lost my older brother the summer before I went to 10th grade. It was devastating for me. Police invading our home in the middle of the night was scary, as they had their guns drawn. My entire family was at gunpoint. The blue lights and red lasers were blinding. As fast as they intruded, my older brother was gone. My parents were blindsided and had no idea what was happening or why my brother was arrested. I felt my parents were still wanting to control us and protect us but feeling it was too late. We had to attend my dad's church, and with our parents working a lot more now, I had freedom outside of Sunday service.

Journal Prompts:

HOW DID READING THIS CHAPTER MAKE YOU FEEL?

DO YOU VIEW LONELINESS AS A GOOD THING OR BAD THING? WHY?

DO YOU TRUST YOURSELF ENOUGH TO BE COMFORTABLE IN YOUR LONLENESS?

DOES YOUR FUNDAMENTAL BELIEF ALLOW FOR YOU TO FEEL COMFORT IN YOUR LONELINESS?

Weekly Journal

Weekly Journal

THEME

Loneliness & Faith

INSIGHT

Overcoming feelings of the negative loneliness starts with the faith that being by yourself is okay.

ADVICE

Ways to stop feeling lonely
1. Acknowledge and accept your feelings about it.
2. Search for and try activities that make interest you. 3. Practice self-care, this can help you connect with yourself.
4. Reach out to your loved ones.

GOAL

Encourage readers to be comfortable with themselves and their spaces.

" Sometimes you need to be alone. Not to be lonely, but to enjoy your free time being yourself."
~Unknown

Blue Amber

Amber (1)

A POWERFUL HEALER AND CLEANSER OF THE BODY, MIND, AND SPIRIT.

By the end of summer, I decided to quit smoking. I came home after being gone all weekend with friends. My mother was sitting on the couch she had reupholstered. When I entered the door and she saw it was me, there was relief. As she continued to watch me, she knew I had been out with friends all weekend. I saw a look of pain and disappointment on my mom's face. For the first time it was directed at me. Never wanting to cause my mom undue pain I vowed to never smoke again. I decided I would quit for my lungs' sake and to make her proud. By this time, my younger sister had confirmed her way out. In retrospect, my sister leaving at a young age likely saved her and kept her sane. She applied and was accepted to attend a boarding school for high school. She spent all four years there. So, I lost my younger sister at the end of summer. My older sister was already in and out.

So, 10th grade was just me again. The other Black families moved away from the area. I was isolated again at school. At home I no longer had the same level of support. My older brother was in jail, my younger sister was away at boarding school, my older sister was not always around either, and my dad never moved back in once my mom healed. They finalized their divorce. It was mostly me, my mom, and my younger brother when he was not with my dad.

Sophomore year, I turned to religion. I started to read the Bible and to write my older brother encouraging letters to help him pass his time in jail. I listened to my dad's sermons and really started praying. I looked up to my grandmother who was heavily involved in church. I also listened to the radio a lot. I learned the lyrics to a lot of oldies but goodies too. I took down my Tupac shrine and started learning more about cooking and baking. I discovered I was better at baking food than using the stovetop. Sophomore year of high school was dry and uneventful. I knew people but was not interested or engaged. My dad helped me get hired for a summer job at the Cleveland MetroParks Rainforest and Zoo as a guest services ticket taker for the summer after my sophomore year.

I was determined to turn my life into something. I learned from the choices of my older siblings. My parents loved how my younger sister was excelling and growing at the boarding school. The results and the difference they noticed in my younger sister were all positive. As a result of her attending boarding school, my parents decided it was best to send me too. 5th grade through sophomore year in high school were the toughest years of my life. At the time, I did not know these were indeed the hardest years of my life. I stayed hopeful throughout all the changes and all the losses.

For years, I suffered with some good times sprinkled in, but mostly I encountered loss after loss. My family was divided after moving from Cleveland. I never imagined things turning out the way our lives unfolded. We never talked about the losses we suffered. I grew up thinking loss was death. Who am I to compare loss and grieving to that of death? Since my nuclear family were all here, living and breathing, I never realized I was in mourning. Still, I did not want to relocate to Indiana to attend a boarding school. I was upset with my parents for the first three weeks I was at the boarding school.

By the time classes started, however, I got over it by telling myself I would make the best of any situation I was faced with. Turns out, attending the boarding school with my younger sister was one of the best decisions made for me. I was entering a network that would prepare me for leadership and college excellence. I made friends and bonded with people different than myself. I actually engaged with others and was excited about my future. Boarding school allowed me to feel close and connected, which was something that I had denied myself in middle school and my first two years of high school. Here, I had to be myself. I did not have to put on a fake smile and pretend I fit in, because I lived with the same people who I attended class with and ate with. We were around each other all the time and became family. I could not hide parts of myself from friends here, because there was nowhere to hide. Junior and senior year, I learned how to navigate a predominantly white institution (PWI). Before junior year I only survived being in a PWI. At boarding school, I came out of my shell and thrived as a result. I made life-long connections during my last two years of high school.

I was happy to reunite with my younger sister at the boarding school. My relationship with my sister continued where we left off like no time apart had passed. We were roommates the two years I attended the school before graduating. I left my younger brother and felt concern for him, as he is eight years younger than me. He pretty much grew up as an only child. He was smart, funny, and protective of us, his sisters. He would go on to live with my dad and his new wife in South Euclid or Richmond Heights. He, too, was excelling in school.

During long weekends and winter breaks when my sister and I would go back to visit Cleveland, I knew my younger brother was good with living with my dad, his wife, and her daughter. We were part of a blended family for the first time, but not for the last time. Our new sister was also in high school, and she said to us, "There are no steps in this house." Meaning, we are family now that our parents married, and we would go on to call each other sister, not stepsisters. I accepted that my dad had moved on. I had two homes to visit when returning to Cleveland for school breaks. My mom's home and my dad's. For me it was a non-issue that my dad remarried. I was open to being in a blended family, plus I was only around for summers and school breaks. Who was I to interrupt or cause trouble for my dad? My mom was content with her life, and that was enough for me to feel at peace. My mom is not the jealous and malicious kind. As usual, my mother led by example. In my eyes she is the model woman for handling whatever life sends her way with grace and ease. I never saw my mom sweat or get worked up over things. I admired that my mom did the best she could, as she knows she is blessed. I noticed how my mother was not petty and did not attempt to keep us away out of spite or anger towards my dad. This set the tone for me to be accepting of my dad's marriage. I never felt I had to choose one parent over the other.

During breaks I would return to my guest services job at The Rainforest. This allowed me to have extra money for me and my younger sister while at boarding school. Living away from home without our parents is a big deal at age 15 or 16. Living away from home was great preparation for college. Having my younger sister with me made moving away to a different state easier for me. I have many memories of my time spent at the boarding school. I developed my creative skills at this school. To entertain ourselves outside the structured programs offered by the school, we came up with different, unique games. There were times we would play as the Godfather. One of us would be the Godfather and barely speak. The others had to cater to whatever the Godfather wanted. For example, in the cafeteria, the Godfather would use nonverbal communication to direct others to order their food and carry it to the table we sat at with our friends.

The school offered plenty of activities, but during down time is when our personalities shined beyond our uniforms. The individuals I met at this school allowed me to accept myself. We spent all our time together. My friends were family, as we often referred to each other. My friends, including my sister, studied together, slept through chapel, laughed, traveled to each other's homes, played sports, exercised, danced, had spade tournaments, celebrated life, performed on stage together, and so many other things.

When we neared the end of my senior year, I became a little closed off. This was how I coped with knowing I would have to separate from my friends. More than once, I sat by myself during events just to deal with loss in my own way. I thought giving myself space would help prepare me for when my friends were not around after high school. This was probably my first realization of separation anxiety. The end of the year was approaching fast, and I did not know how to deal with the fact that I would no longer have moments like these with my group of friends again. There was a time when we had an event in the auditorium with just the school for girls. I sat away from my friends, and they wanted me to sit with them. I told them no. They teased that I was sitting with my invisible friends. There were at least a couple of other incidents like that. I never had invisible friends, experienced hallucinations, or heard voices. Was I beginning to break down? Were those the beginning signs of something declining with my mental health?

I went on to excel my first year in college. I originally wanted to attend a Historically Black College or University (HBCU) in Louisiana. However, my financial aid package came too late. I accepted an offer to attend a university in Cleveland. I returned to my hometown for undergraduate school. I was the first of my siblings to graduate high school and the first to attend college. My dad purchased me a brand-new Honda Civic as a reward. When I started freshman year at a PWI it felt familiar to my time at Broadview Heights schools. This time around, I countered the isolation by getting involved and engaged. I joined the Dolan Queens flag football team. I joined the multicultural office group for minority students. I stayed on campus freshman year. I lived in an all-girls dorm. I started out pre-med major.

That first year of college I thought I was doing everything right. I volunteered at a hospital for one of my classes. I was placed in the children's wing. I was to clean their toys and walk to their rooms to see if they wanted to play games. Once, I walked into the room and a staff member was in with the child. I asked if they wanted to play a game. The staff member said, "No, you two play." As the staff member walked by me to exit the room, she said, "I'm so glad you came in here, I was running out of things to say." I knew I would bring the kids joy and encouragement. The impact was the opposite. Some of the children in hospital clothes were bedridden. These kids dealing with their ailments mustered up a smile when they saw me. They were tenacious. I was forever impacted in a positive way. Here I was, healthy all my life, never spending a night in a hospital bed. Volunteering in the kid's wing changed my outlook and made me appreciative for all I had. For all my full experiences in life, I was grateful. Externally, on the surface, I smiled and was happy.

After volunteering at the hospital, I found joy. I tapped into the core of who I am. I learned that my circumstance did not have to define my attitude. Yes, there were times I was told to sing and attend Bible study at nursing homes. I was exposed to the sick in that setting with the church and bringing communion to the sick and shut-in with my dad for his church. This was different. To see the youth still with sparks in their eyes in the hospital touched my soul. I decided to focus on academics but to take it easy on myself and to enjoy my life more. Before freshman year, I knew I wanted to become a pediatrician. I needed more experience working with kids. I thought instead of returning to guest services at the Rainforest for my summer job, I would learn more working at a camp.

A month or two prior to summer, I went to the office of career services at my university. I started the application process with local camps referred to me by the career service representatives. They also helped me write and prepare my resume. During the resume writing, application submission, and interview process, I realized I enjoyed the process. It was simple to me, and I learned of the field called human resources. I talked with my advisor regularly, and he knew I was pre-med, but I asked him about HR. I inquired how I could enter that field as my major or as a minor. He told me about two options. I could switch to the business school and graduate maybe a year late. Or I could go the psychology route. After talking with him more he mapped out the classes I would need to make the switch to Psychology. Now, my mom told me if I went the psychology route to go on to become a psychiatrist. My mother told me that completing the path to become a doctor was the best option if I wanted a career path. I listened to my mom but went on to commit to study Industrial Organizational Psychology which would allow me to work in human resources right after completing undergraduate school. I changed direction at the end of freshman year.

Journal Prompts:

HOW DID READING THIS CHAPTER MAKE YOU FEEL?

WHAT DOES YOUR HAPPINESS MEAN TO YOU?

WHAT ARE THINGS THAT MAKE YOU FEEL AT PEACE?

DO YOU HAVE THE ABILITY TO ACCEPT, OR MAKE PEACE WITH THE THINGS THAT HAVE CAUSED YOU STRESS?

Weekly Journal

Weekly Journal

THEME

Choosing Peace & Life

INSIGHT

The protection of your own peace comes with self-made boundaries. This is you choose your own life.

ADVICE

Ways to choose peace
1. Find friendship in you.
2. Practice empathy for yourself and others
3. Validate yourself.
4. Live with decisions

GOAL

Encourage readers to choose peace, which in hind-sight is choosing life.

" Choosing stillness in the midst of chaos is the path toward living in peace"
~Unknown

Blue Amber

Amber (2)

CONSIDERED THE "SOUL OF THE TIGER." IT WAS CARRIED FOR PROTECTION AND THOUGHT TO BALANCE EMOTIONS.

After completing biology, I was not confident about the chemistry courses I would need to complete sophomore year. So, I changed gears. Now I realize my mom's option was best. At the time, I did not understand that I did not need to have straight A's in my classes. I needed only to pass my classes even if I had C's. Studies show that B and C students connect better with their patients, as their social skills are better suited to listen to the patient. Had I stayed the course like my mom suggested I would be a doctor now. Instead of listening to her I went the "easier" route and registered for the I/O Psychology program. I do not have regrets, but I may have been a doctor by now.

Summer came, and I interviewed and hired for a job as a camp counselor. Before the kids arrived at camp, the staff met and stayed at the camp for a week. That week was fun. We learned all the games and rules. I felt like a child again. I was reminded of when my family would go camping. My parents would take us in my grandparents' motorhome to the campgrounds. Now I was being paid to camp, something I used to do for fun. For this job, I learned how to make fire with sticks and other earth elements. I listened to stories shared by the camp staff, ate the food at the camp, and just bonded with the staff. We had to play all the games and walk around the campgrounds to learn our way around. My assignment was archery. I had taken archery in high school gym class, so I had the most experience with it. That week with just staff went by fast, as I was having so much fun. We had the weekend off. I went home, and that Sunday I attended my dad's church. At the time, he was preaching at Mt. Moriah. That Sunday, I do not know what he preached about. All I know is I was in tears the entire service, as I felt like I was disappointing my father because that separation from and pressure of turning my back on the church was a lot to bear. I cried hard, too, and I was not big on crying. My cousin Melody was in service that Sunday, and she told me I was a cry baby and kept asking what was wrong. I kept telling her, "I do not know why I am crying so much and so hard." I was to return to the camp the next day. My sisters dropped me off at camp happily because they would have my car for the summer.

The kids arrived at camp a few hours after the staff. I was ready, but nervous for some reason. The first day went well. Tuesday was a long day and we started activities with the kids. I played in the pool and fished with the kids. I felt like a big kid, as I enjoyed the activities and games as much as them. I taught them archery as best and safely as I could. The kids must have bonded with me more than I knew, as they began to tell me their stories. These were not happy stories about their home lives. The kids came from rough backgrounds. I wanted to help the kids, but did not have the words, as we were not to talk about religion to the kids. I felt overwhelmed by the stories, and I asked another camp counselor how she was handling things. She shared that she, too, had a hard upbringing, as her mom passed away when she was young. She told me she went through a lot herself, and as a result she has tough skin. Well, I wanted to offer resources to the kids but did not have the means or ideas on where to start helping. Knowing what the kids struggled with was overwhelming for me.

One night at the campfire, I was sitting on the log staring into the fire for a long time. One of the other counselors came to me and asked if I was okay, because I looked out of it. Later that night there was a bad thunderstorm. Lightning and heavy rain kept me up. I was frightened for some reason, and I could not sleep. I woke up one of the other counselors in my tent and asked her to pray with me. She did, and I went to my bed and finally fell asleep. Morning finally arrived. I did not eat breakfast that morning, but I told the kids at my table to say their blessings and enjoy breakfast. I knew something was not right with me, as we were not to discuss or encourage religion. I had not brought up prayer before that morning. I called my dad to come get me from the camp that morning. I did not know what was wrong with me. Is this what my mom went through? Was I having a panic attack? Why were my thoughts not clear? Was I dehydrated?

My dad rushed to pick me up and took me to my grandmother's, then later to the emergency room. Since I did not continue talking or eating and I was not functioning as I normally did, my dad decided to take me to the hospital. I was not aware of why my mind was doing this. I knew what was happening around me, but the overstimulation of the drive to the hospital caused me to decline more. I was in a trance, and by the time my siblings and mom made it to the ER I was close to full catatonia. I was moving slowly, and I was not talking. I recall seeing my siblings and wanting to say something to them, only my words did not come out. I said each of their names in my mind as I reached out to each of them. Only my younger brother was unable to make to the ER. All were very concerned for my wellbeing.

I was admitted to a hospital for the first time at the age of 18. Was it dehydration and exhaustion? Maybe both. Hours later, when I was transferred by ambulance from the ER to a hospital, I woke up in a psych ward. What others think is the worst thing had happened to me. Ever since 7th grade, in the back of my mind, I wondered if I was going to go insane. My cousin later joked that the kids at that camp drove me crazy. While in the hospital my family would visit and bring me food. I sang on the phone to my younger brother the Akon song "I'm locked up they won't let me out" and we laughed.

There was a time I was in the bathroom at the hospital, and I do not know for how long. When I exited the bathroom, the lady I shared the room with said to me, "You were in there for a long a** time. What were you doing?"

I said, "Looking in the mirror."

She then told me I was going to speak in front of a lot of people one day. She asked why I was not talking, and I shrugged my shoulders. She went on to tell me how I just walk up and down the hallway with my head held high. She observed how I kept my chin up even when at my low point in the psych ward. I knew exactly what she was talking about, as in my mind I was thinking about my father who told me to always walk tall. He said, "Hold your head high and be proud." As I walked that hallway, I replayed his advice and kept my head up.

Now, I never knew why the lady said I would speak in front of a lot of people one day, but I received her statement and the positivity she was giving me. I still think about her statement and wonder if I will one day speak for others in front of a lot of people.

When my mom came to visit, she showed me how to shower without direct contact with the floor. I was afraid to put my bare feet on the bathroom floor. I refused to shower until she showed me a trick. I was to put the towel halfway in the shower and leave the other half on the bathroom floor as a way of not having my bare feet touch. Shower shoes were not permitted at the time. Being in a psych ward for the first time was confusing for me. All the nurses, assistants or techs, and activity facilitators made it difficult for me to keep track of who was who. I had to attend groups. Groups were activity time and being social in group or participating was a ticket out of the psych ward. I did not catch on to it my first time in the hospital, but the more you talk with staff the more likely you are to leave quickly. Well, I was catatonic by the time I reached the ward.

The process of going from the ER to a bed is an overwhelming thing. I was already in a fragile state. I was afraid for my life and that of my nuclear family. So much so I was essentially paralyzed. Not talking, eating, drinking, or moving. My thoughts were going a mile a minute and I was terrified. So, to have doctors and nurses trying to do intake was petrifying. They were likely afraid of hurting or worsening my condition. I was to take off my clothes to put on hospital gowns. Normally, I was uncomfortable undressing in front of teammates and roommates. These strangers called techs and nurses trying to make me more comfortable was darn near impossible with the state of fear I felt. The time it takes to find an open bed for a patient is extensive and prolonged by what my medical insurance will or will not cover. Once in the ER they draw blood and lots of it to test for everything. Going through this process with strangers was scary and to me unnecessary, as I was there for my brain. Later I learned there is a period of observation in the ER. However long that takes, I do not know. They also sometimes had to wait for the on-call psych doctor to arrive. All these delays for treatment made my condition worse. The noises, the bright lights, the myriad of nurses, techs, doctors, and patients causing overstimulation in the ER is ridiculous for a person trying to maintain mental stability.

After being released from the hospital, I spent the rest of the summer after freshman year healing. It was not easy because of the side effects. I took the medicine as prescribed, but it took weeks for me to feel somewhat like myself. I made up my mind that, like my mom, I, too, would overcome this obstacle. She influenced me greatly by her actions. It was not any one thing she said, it was her example. This minor setback would not define me. As I mentioned earlier in my writing, it took me two decades to rebuild confidence and my self-esteem.

I was determined to finish my education and make something out of my life. First semester of sophomore year I returned to school at my university. I stayed on campus again. I did not have a roommate until the middle of the semester. I was medicated at age 18.

I attempted suicide for the first and last time in my dorm room sophomore year. It was a Saturday morning. I took my belt and tied it around my neck. I tried to hang myself from the towel rack. The towel rack was on the door to my dorm room. It was nailed to the lower section of the door, so about halfway down on the door. I tied the other part of the belt to the towel rack. Obviously, I failed. I did not want to die. I was suffering a side effect of the medicine that was meant to help me. Suicidal thoughts are a side effect of the medication. I only shared this with my older sister. I mentioned before she has a dark sense of humor. Thankfully, we can laugh about how my attempt was the safest attempt ever. I was able to just untie my belt. I learned to laugh at my pain, as Kevin Hart says. I acknowledged that we all have breaking points and limits. That was my lowest point. As I hurt, I hoped, like Amanda Gorman put it.

I no longer wanted to take medicine. It seemed it was more harmful than helpful. I suffered other side effects like weight gain and involuntary eye movement. Involuntary eye movement causes my eyes to roll and move uncontrollably. It is painful and honestly still causes me fear that they will become stuck. I worked with the psychiatrist to titrate off the medicine. I believed I was better and did not need it anymore. I was wrong. I was better because of the medicine. When I went off the medicine, I ended up back in the hospital. This time I had insomnia, I felt overwhelmed with life, and I was paranoid that bad things were lurking. I took my health in my own hands after taking off my second semester of sophomore year in college.

During my recovery I had support from my family, my sisters especially. They never made me feel I was different or forgotten about. My younger sister even drove in the middle of a blizzard from Ohio to Illinois to pick me up. I was in and out of touch with reality and as a result was misinterpreting my environment. I felt I wanted everything to stop moving as my thoughts were coming in faster than I could process them. Racing thoughts led to my decreased mobility. I was overthinking my every move and it was crippling, as I literally could not move. My sister's roommate rode with her to get me from a friend's university I had flown to visit. By the time they arrived at Peoria campus I was out of it. My dad had told me not to go and that I had not made it to 100% or even 85% recovery. Later, after returning from that trip, I began to listen more to my family's advice about the condition I deal with.

That spring, I will never forget when my dad took me for a walk at Garfield Metroparks. He pointed out the trees and how they were straight at the base. He went on to say, "Notice how the trees towards the top are curved and have bends."

I said, "Yes, I see that."

He explained how the trees had to move and adjust when they started out. They had to be flexible during their first years to move in the direction of the sun. To find that optimum light for their survival, they needed to posture themselves to stand out. If the trees did not move or bend to reach the sunlight, they may not have survived. As the tree ages it straightens out, as it is solid, grounded and postured to stand straight. During that walk I found that being in nature made me feel more at ease.

Journal Prompts:

HOW DID READING THIS CHAPTER MAKE YOU FEEL?

WHAT IS ONE THING THAT CAUSED YOU STRESS OR ANXIETY THIS WEEK?

HAS THE SITUATION BEEN RESOLVED? IF NOT, REFER TO THE ANXIETY TECHNIQUES AND COME BACK AND JOURNAL.

Weekly Journal

Weekly Journal

THEME

Anxiety Solutions

INSIGHT

Gaining control of one's stresses and anxiety can be a huge relief.

ADVICE

Ways to help alleviate feelings of anxiety.
1. Stay active
2. Practice Mindfulness
3. Practice deep breath ing.
4.Prioritize self-care

GOAL

Encourage readers to gain knowledge on anxiety solutions.

"Do not let your difficulties fill you with anxiety, after all it is only in the darkest nights that stars shine more brightly"
~Ali Ibn Abi Talib

Blue Amber

Yellow Amber

FOUND AROUND THE WORLD AND RECOMMENDED WHEN YOU WANT A FLOW OF GOOD FORTUNE.

I met with a psychiatrist; my parents were there with me for the outpatient appointment. She was Black. I was excited, as it was my first encounter with a Black professional in the field. She asked me what I wanted to do. I told her I wanted to finish my education. I had a choice to stay on pharmaceuticals or try natural remedies. No guarantees that either option would work. The natural remedies were a bigger gamble for me because of the financial cost. I had given my savings to my mom for her to make a down payment on her house. I did not have the funds for natural remedies. Natural solutions are not covered by insurance. I decided to continue taking medicine. It took months for my body to adjust to the pills. I would sleep sometimes 12 to 13 hours straight. The fatigue was real. The medicine increased my appetite. Eating and sleeping so much created weight gain. A lot of times if I stood up too quickly, I would get dizzy and have to hold on to a wall or squat to prevent myself from passing out. I switched medicines a couple of times because some of the side effects were intolerable for me. One brand called Invega caused me to jerk violently and uncontrollably at random times. Geodon was the medicine I settled on until I found out about Abilify. Working with a nurse practitioner, I began to couple the medicine with Cogentin to help reduce the side effects. Of course, Cogentin has its own set of side effects. For me, it caused dry mouth. I continued to take it, as dry mouth is better than the involuntary muscle movement.

As time passed my mind healed from the extreme fear, and the catatonic behavior subsided. I was able to reduce the high dosage of medicine. This decreased the fatigue and lethargic feeling, as well as some of the dry mouth. I returned to school in the summer. I took classes at my university and another local college that summer to catch up. I started back full time at my university during the fall of my junior year. I continued to study I/O Psychology. I had family to hang out with and to offer support. I felt close to normal again being around my blended family. When I left sophomore year 2nd semester, I could have given up. However, to give up is not an option. To keep going is all I knew to do. To keep going was the example my mom set for me. I decided back in high school that I would make her proud. My mom did not really have that mouthpiece, but her example and actions speak volumes. I kept going because I had no reason to stop. I remember the joy the kids in the hospital gave me.

"Who am I to not press on towards the mark?" as my dad says in his sermons. I used to think about all the gospel songs and all the people who say I almost lost my mind. As if to say losing your mind is the worst. Maybe for some, it is. However, the loss of a loved one who is still breathing is the worst for me. I now think to myself, I lost my mind, and I am still going. Yes, I was on disability. I did not drop out pregnant like classmates thought. I made sure I kept up with my doctor's appointments and made it to therapy sessions in addition to classes and studying. I learned of the Students With Disabilities Office my senior year of undergrad. I used their services once, as I was not aware of everything offered.

I went on to graduate with my class. Completing undergraduate school at a Jesuit school was no easy feat. Doing so took courage. I had to make up my mind about what I wanted to do. Once I made up my mind, I went for it with no excuses. I did not mope around feeling sorry for myself. My grandfather would say: "When you fall down in the mud do not stay there and waddle in it, get up and keep going." That is not to say I did not have bad days, but where is the rainbow with no sun and rain? How do you appreciate the good without the bad? I learned to never take away tomorrow in response to today.

I live a full life, yet I am a work in progress. I continue to commit to being a life-long learner. I think my curiosity keeps me intrigued about what is next.

Journal Prompts:

HOW DID READING THIS CHAPTER MAKE YOU FEEL?

WHAT IS THE BIGGEST OBSTACLE YOU HAVE FACED IN YOUR LIFE?

HOW HAVE YOU OVERCOME IT?

WHO CAN YOU GO TO, TO ENCOURAGE YOU O PERSERVERE?

Weekly Journal

Weekly Journal

THEME

Perserverance

INSIGHT

One of the key values of perseverance is the ability to keep going despite the challenge you may be facing. Always remember to just keep going.

ADVICE

Ways to persevere
1. Accept changes
2. Remove all self-doubt.
3. Maintain your optimism.
4. Keep persisting.

GOAL

Show readers what it means to persevere.

"Success is not final, failure is not fatal: it is the courage to continue that counts."
~Winston Churchill

Blue Amber

Amber (3)

A STONE OF MANIFESTATION

Summer 2005, I began working a fulltime job in Human Resources with a Fortune 500 company. It took over a year for me to find employment and I felt discouraged, like education was not worth it. On the other hand, being out of work for a year gave me plenty of time to work on my mental health. I went to a temp agency after having minimal luck finding employment after graduation. I was to fill in for a lady going on maternity leave. She decided to remain a fulltime mom, and the company hired me full time. In the fall of 2005, I purchased a condominium in a suburb of Cleveland. Owning my own home at age 23 felt amazing. I had become a responsible adult despite it all. November 2005, I took my first overseas trip. During Thanksgiving season, I went to visit my younger sister in Taiwan. Once she graduated from her university, she went to teach English in Taiwan. I used a credit card to purchase my flight. I still have the card open to this day and it has contributed to my credit score. I am so glad I purchased the flight on the card. I maxed out the card but worked diligently to pay down the balance. My job at The Rainforest required direct deposit. I had to open an account and balance a checkbook as a teenager. Being a responsible teen who valued discipline paid off for me in ways I never dreamed. Purchasing a home at age 23 was a huge accomplishment.

Going overseas was one of the best decisions in my life. I took the long flight not knowing what to expect when I landed. I was excited though. I knew my sister would be there waiting just as happy to see me. I felt safe in Taiwan. It rained a lot there, but the monsoon season did not stop us from visiting different sites and going out. She would go on to live and teach in Costa Rica. I was a fan of travel and wanted more stamps on my passport, so I was happy to plan my vacation to Costa Rica to visit my sister. The trip to Costa Rica was well worth it too. The flavors, the sun, the colors, warm water, and nature were all around me and I loved it. I continued to work and looked forward to my next adventure.

My coworker and now unofficial mentor told me one day, "Amber, you need mirror time, a lot of mirror time." I understood that she meant I needed to believe in myself and to learn my worth. She was telling me what my parents painted on my brother's wall at our home in Cleveland...to "know thyself" and "be true to thyself." She essentially said *put in the work to know that I am everything and then some*. My coworker watered the self-esteem and confidence seeds my parents planted. She saw my worth more than I did at that time.

Now looking back, I see the fear I felt that night when I was safe at home surrounded by those who will do most anything for me, making it past my fear to go to the bathroom that night

I had to go on my own. My family could not do this one thing for me. The one thing is they cannot have confidence and healthy self-esteem for me. I had to muster up courage on my own and had to believe in myself. The fear was not real. Had I taken the time to look I would have seen a beautiful reflection of myself in the glass window on the door across from the bathroom. That night I had to step out in darkness to get to the light. I had to stop feeding into the fear I was creating. I fought my fear to accomplish my goal and made it to the light. I will always have fear; I am never absent of it, but I move despite the fear.

It took me a long time to come around to seeing my worth and to press on even though I was afraid. The only thing constant is change. If those trees I spoke of earlier did not posture themselves to receive optimum sunlight, they may have stunted their growth. We as humans are meant to move. The earth literally moves. To stay still, to freeze, to be stuck is literally and figuratively killing you.

My high school friends were at a talent show one day at boarding school. There were only two performances. My sister, friends, and I performed on stage as the N-tations. We did a dance to The Temptations' "Beauty is Only Skin Deep" and then mixed in a dance to an NSYNC song. The other performer sang a song by herself. The lyrics' chorus was "we got to keep on moving." She lost the talent show to us. However, her message rings so clear now. My friends and I still think about how relevant her song is.

I started graduate school while working fulltime, and I earned my MBA in 2008. I always wanted to study abroad during undergrad. I never did because I was afraid of my health and because of finances. When the opportunity to travel with my graduate school presented itself, I jumped at the chance. I traveled to South Africa and Zambia with classmates, two professors, and a family friend. I visited a waterfall larger than Niagara Falls. One of the seven wonders of the world, Victoria Falls was enormous. As if seeing the falls itself was not breathtaking enough I bungee jumped from a bridge near the falls. I did not have any mental health disruptions throughout my tenure working and traveling. I was excited about life and my big, blended family was proud when I graduated from grad school. On those long flights overseas, I had envisioned a life of travel for myself and my siblings. I knew if I could overcome my setbacks like my mom, that my other siblings could too. There were times where I wished they, too, were able to experience the overseas trips with me. I remind myself it is not too late.

After years of working for the same company, earning my master's degree, and not advancing quickly enough in my career, I wanted a change. I was not moving up the corporate ladder like I envisioned I would. There was not much room for growth in the human resources department of the company I worked with. My manager was in her late 30's, and the director was not leaving anytime soon either. I was comfortable but should have looked for other opportunities outside of my company. It was not long after the financial crisis in 2008 that I decided I would move overseas. A family friend emailed me a program to look into. It was a graduate school program where I could earn a master's degree while teaching English in China. I applied to the program at a university in California. In 2011, I was accepted and left my job for California and China. I lived on campus in California for eight weeks of courses including Mandarin lessons. Then I moved to China with the cohort for the master's program.

I had an easy time transitioning to China, and my entrance to Hangzhou was smooth. China was different from the US, as the overwhelming majority of the people were Asian, whereas in America, walking down a street or being in a mall or store you saw diversity. In China I could go days without seeing non-Asian people. The food in China was different from Chinese food served in America. I had traditional Chinese food in China and there were no fortune cookies at any of the restaurants I dined at. Common restaurants in America were a luxury in China. For example, Pizza Hut and McDonalds were considered fancy in China.

I was abroad with a cohort of American students. I taught college students at a university in XiaXia. There were several universities in the area, which was beneficial for me because the college students spoke some English. This made my transition and adjustment easier than being surrounded by non-English speakers. I learned a little Mandarin, the essentials like food, directions, and greetings. Had I continued to mingle with the locals and not the expats, I would have learned to speak and read more Mandarin. I started getting homesick and hanging out more with those fluent in English.

The Chinese welcomed me. Taxi drivers would yell out "Obama," as he was President then. I took it as a compliment for them to use the English they knew and that they recognized I was American and were excited to have me in their country. I definitely did stand out in China. I know the times I would wear my hair in a curly fro, my students were in awe. To be that close to me with different textured hair amazed my students. It reminded them how I was different. I still hear the gasping whoas the students would let out when I entered the room with my curly fro. It was in a good way. Not like when I entered the room as the only Black person back in middle school. Here I was older, but also knew I could be myself. I did not feel I was being judged for being Black, but I was setting an example for my people. I represented Black women but in a natural way. It was not the same pressure as it was at home in the USA. In the USA when I am the only Black woman in the room there is pressure to prove I belong in the room. With the students here, they were curious in an innocent and endearing way.

During our long winter break for Chinese New Year, I traveled with a good friend. She and I were roommates while in California. We visited Hong Kong, Thailand, Macau, Philippines, and other cities in China including Harbin and Guangzhou. These experiences traveling were amazing. I may not have made it through without my friend, travel buddy, and roommate. The students in my cohort were there for me in a way I can never repay them for.

After traveling when winter break ended, I became ill in China. Yes, I lost my mind overseas. I was with a friend who was in China from Mexico, and we went to eat with a staff member from my cohort. They knew I was not stable. We made it to a Pizza Hut and sat down. We ordered food and I excused myself to go to the bathroom. I was afraid and ended up leaving Pizza Hut. I ran from my friend and the staff member. I made it back to my apartment in XiaXia. My dad had to be a nervous wreck. He and the staff sent two male classmates to my apartment. They were so kind, brought me food, and stayed with me all night. The next morning, they took me to the hospital. Before I went, I called a classmate from high school who was studying to become a psychiatrist. We video chatted for a few minutes, and the two students from my cohort got on camera and told her hello too. We taxied to the hospital. It took a long time for me to be admitted. Most of the students in my cohort who lived in Hangzhou showed up for me. My friend and travel buddy came all the way from Shanghai to see me. I knew it was serious and urgent because she came without makeup on. She never goes anywhere without her makeup on. I tried to pull it together. I was still fearful and kept trying to leave the hospital. My cohort stuck with me until I was admitted into the hospital. Thankfully, my dad and sister orchestrated my return. My dad had coached my classmates on how to work with me while I was in a different state of mind. I know it was devastating for everyone to see me this way, but especially for my dad. The other times I became ill in the US, he and my mom had been around to ensure I received proper treatment. This time, he was only able to communicate over the phone.

In the Chinese hospital I calmed down when they gave me medication. When I entered the ward, I kept screaming that I did not want to die. I remember vividly what happened, however I did not have control to behave like myself. I recall what happened and how I behaved, but the reason for the behavior I cannot explain. The cohort staff member had to be frightened, experiencing my drastic behavior firsthand.

No one on the floor spoke English. By morning, I was more relaxed. I played table tennis with one of the Chinese patients. I ate food that my hospital roommate brought to me after going out with her family. Two of my students came to visit me in the hospital as well. My friend from Mexico came to visit me and brought me food and clothes. The fear I felt had diminished by then. My dad was working to have me transferred from the Hangzhou hospital to a hospital in Shanghai where the staff spoke English. He called his connections in Columbus to have the US Ambassador visit me in the Shanghai hospital. While there, I was not eating the food prepared. Someone sent me a bunch of bananas. I smashed them, and I laugh to myself at the irony of being bananas eating bananas in China. Thanks to whomever sent the fruit.

I had elected and paid for international health insurance through the university. In Shanghai, I told my younger sister how I wanted to come home. I gave her the insurance information over the phone and told her a traveling nurse was covered to fly with me. I received great care in China but was happy I was going home to my family. Sometimes though, I wonder how it would have turned out if I had stayed and healed in Asia.

On the flight back to the US, I wrote a note to the only Black flight attendant telling her to smile, it would be okay. They wondered who I was flying with first class from Asia. The flight attendant I gave the encouraging note to came and asked me who I was traveling with. I told her it was my nurse. She smiled. This is significant to me because I feel I inspired her in the same way the kids in the hospital I volunteered for had changed me. She was clearly having a bad day. I believe her perspective of a bad day changed.

Journal Prompts:

HOW DID READING THIS CHAPTER MAKE YOU FEEL?

ARE YOU CHASING PROGRESSION OR PERFECTION?

WHATT DOES THE BEST VERSION OF YOUR LIFE LOOK LIKE?

WHAT STEPS WILL YOU TAKE TO GET THERE?

Weekly Journal

Weekly Journal

THEME

Self-Fulfillment

INSIGHT

You can be who you are. Whatever you envision your life to be, you can achieve.

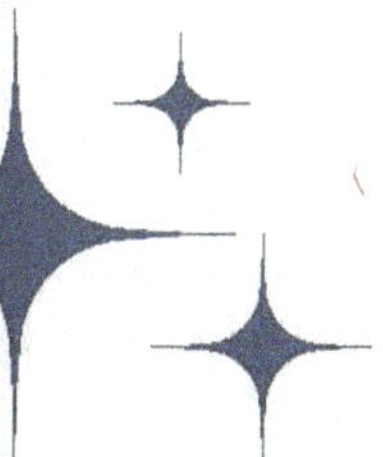

GOAL

To acknowledge your end goal can be happiness

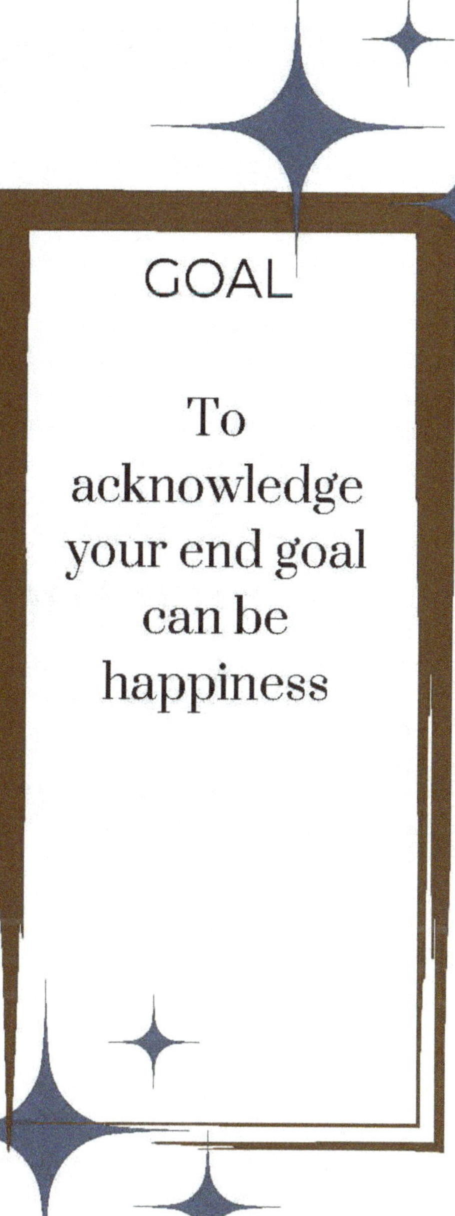

ADVICE

Ways to achieve fulfillment

1. Do things you love.
2. Imagine the best.
3. Challenge yourself to grow
4. Be mindful and present

"Purpose, joy and inner peace are the only status symbols worth having."
~Anthon St. Maarten

Blue Amber

Acknowledgements

I thank myself, for finding the courage to write about the parts of my life that I was embarrassed to speak about for two decades. Countless thanks to my parents for never giving up on me, even to this day. Many thanks to my siblings, both biological and those gained through marriage. By just being yourselves, you have encouraged me to do the same.

Thanks for the healing power of laughter and the relieving power of tears. I am grateful for all my friends near and far; for those who were informed and for those who I did not share my struggle with. I appreciate the support from the AME church family and the network of schools I have attended.

To nurses, hospital staff, doctors, and nurse practitioners who have worked with me over the years, thanks.

Lastly, big shout out of thanks to the editors and my coach for helping me through the writing process.

Bio

Amber Snyder was born and raised in Cleveland, Ohio. After graduating with a Bachelor of Science degree in Psychology and a focus on Industrial/Organizational Psychology Amber began working for a Fortune 500 company. She also earned a Master of Business Administration with a focus on Human Resources from Baldwin Wallace University.

After years in the private sector, Amber decided to teach overseas in China at China Jiliang University while she earned a Master of Arts in International Studies. Amber's career has continued to grow and flourish as she has worked in both private and government organizations.

Amber's vision is to create avenues for communication and improvements in the health sector for disadvantaged communities. She lives a soft life and is a certified personal trainer.

To connect with Amber for speaking opportunities, you can reach her at: a@glifellc.org

www.ingramcontent.com/pod-product-compliance
Lightning Source LLC
LaVergne TN
LVHW081416110826
845149LV00010B/1764

* 9 7 9 8 9 8 8 7 0 5 2 0 8 *